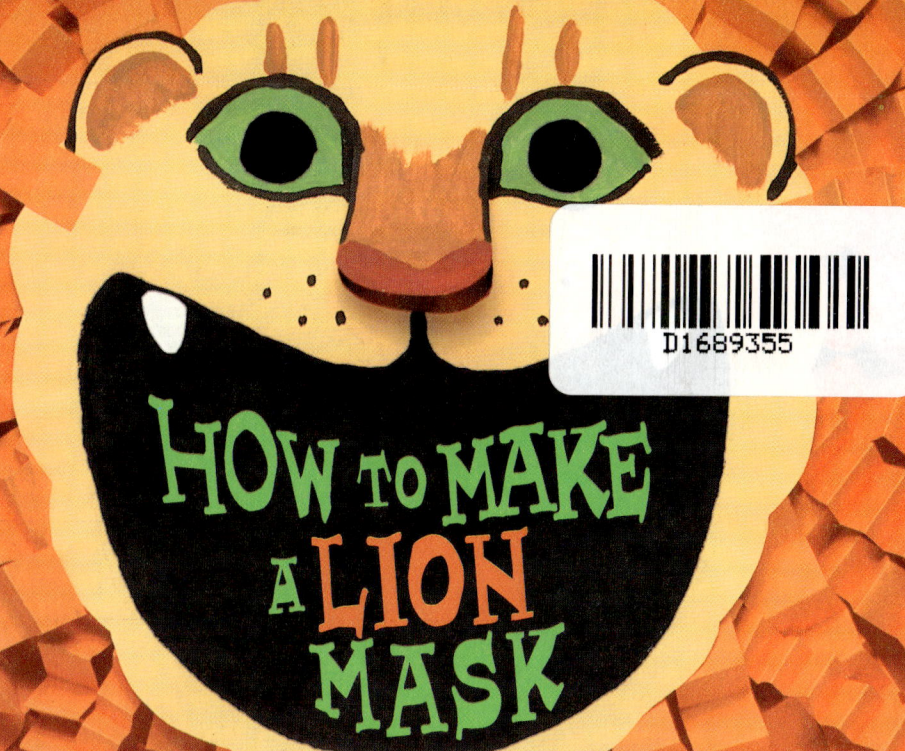

HOW TO MAKE A LION MASK

by Hannah Markley

photos by Tracey Wheeler
art by Mary Lynn Carson

HARCOURT BRACE & COMPANY
Orlando   Atlanta   Austin   Boston   San Francisco   Chicago   Dallas   New York
Toronto   London

If you go to the animal fair,

If you wear a mask, nobody will know it's you.

Here is a lion mask that you can make. It can be scary or sad or happy.

You decide what kind of lion mask it will be.

First, get all of the things you will need.

Use the pattern on these pages to make your mask. Trace this pattern onto paper.

Then cut out the lion pattern.
Don't forget the eyes and nose.

Now use the pattern to trace your mask. Draw lines so you know where to cut.

When you have cut it out, color and decorate your mask neatly.

Glue the stick onto the mask.

And try it on.

Now do your biggest roar so everybody can hear you.